Also by Jaroslaw Jankowski

Why Are We So Different?
Your Guide to the 16 Personality Types

Why are we so very different from one another? Why do we organise our lives in such disparate ways? Why are our modes of assimilating information so varied? Why are our approaches to decision-making so diverse? Why are our forms of relaxing and 'recharging our batteries' so dissimilar?

Your Guide to the 16 Personality Types will help you to understand both yourselves and other people better. It will aid you not only in avoiding any number of traps, but also in making the most of your personal potential, as well as in taking the right decisions about your education and career and in building healthy relationships with others. The book contains the ID16™© Personality Test, which will enable you to determine your own personality type. It also offers a comprehensive description of each of the sixteen types.

The Administrator

Your Guide
to the ESTJ Personality Type

The ID16^{TM©} *Personality Types series*

JAROSLAW JANKOWSKI
M.Ed., EMBA

LOGOS
MEDIA

This is a book which can help you exploit your potential more fully, build healthy relationships with other people and make the right decisions about your education and career. However, it should not be considered to be a substitute for expert physiological or psychiatric consultation. Neither the author nor the publisher accept any responsibility whatsoever for any detrimental effects which may result from the inappropriate use of this book.

ID16™© is an independent typology developed by Polish educator and manager Jaroslaw Jankowski and grounded in Carl Gustav Jung's theory. It should not be confused with the personality typologies and tests proposed by other authors or offered by other institutions.

Original title: Twój typ osobowości: Administrator (ESTJ)
Translated from the Polish by Caryl Swift
Proof reading: Lacrosse | experts in translation
Layout editing by Zbigniew Szalbot

Published by LOGOS MEDIA

Paperback: ISBN 978-83-7981-048-2
EPUB: ISBN 978-83-7981-049-9
MOBI: ISBN 978-83-7981-050-5

Contents

Contents 5

Preface 7

ID16™© and Jungian Personality Typology 9

The Administrator (ESTJ) 14

    The Personality in a Nutshell 14

    General character traits 16

    Socially 20

    Work and career paths 25

    Potential strengths and weaknesses 30

    Personal development 32

    Well-known figures 35

The ID16™© Personality Types in a Nutshell 37

The Administrator (ESTJ)... 37

The Advocate (ESFJ) 39

The Animator (ESTP)... 40

The Artist (ISFP) 41

The Counsellor (ENFJ) 43

The Director (ENTJ) 44

The Enthusiast (ENFP)... 45

The Idealist (INFP) 47

The Innovator (ENTP)... 48

The Inspector (ISTJ) 50

The Logician (INTP)... 51

The Mentor (INFJ).. 52

The Practitioner (ISTP) 54

The Presenter (ESFP) 55

The Protector (ISFJ)... 57

The Strategist (INTJ).. 58

Additional information... 60

The four natural inclinations.................................... 60

The approximate percentage of each personality
type in the world population.................................... 62

The approximate percentage of women and men
of each personality type in the world
population 63

Bibliography 65

Preface

The work in your hands is a compendium of knowledge on the *administrator*. It forms part of the *ID16™© Personality Types* series, which consists of sixteen books on the individual personality types and *Who Are You? The ID16™© Personality Test*, an introduction to the ID16™© independent personality typology, which is based on the theory developed by Carl Gustav Jung.

As you explore this book on the *administrator*, you will find the answer to a number of crucial questions:

- How do *administrators* think and what do they feel? How do they make decisions? How do they solve problems? What makes them anxious? What do they fear? What irritates them?

- Which personality types are they happy to encounter on their road through life and which ones do they avoid? What kind of friends, life partners and parents do they make? How do others perceive them?
- What are their vocational predispositions? What sort of work environment allows them to function most effectively? Which careers best suit their personality type?
- What are their strengths and what do they need to work on? How can they make the most of their potential and avoid pitfalls?
- Which famous people correspond to the *administrator*'s profile?

The book also contains the most essential information about the ID16™© typology.

We sincerely hope that it will help you in coming to know yourself and others better.

ID16™© and Jungian Personality Typology

ID16™© numbers among what are referred to as Jungian personality typologies, which draw on the theories developed by Carl Gustav Jung (1875-19161), a Swiss psychiatrist and psychologist and a pioneer of the 'depth psychology' approach.

On the basis of many years of research and observation, Jung came to the conclusion that the differences in people's attitudes and preferences are far from random. He developed a concept which is highly familiar to us today: the division of people into extroverts and introverts. In addition, he distinguished four personality functions, which form two opposing pairs: sensing-intuition and thinking-feeling. He also established that one function is dominant in each pair. He became convinced that each and every person's dominant functions are fixed and independent of external conditions and that, together, what they form is a personality type.

In 1938, two American psychiatrists, Horace Gray and Joseph Wheelwright, created the first personality test based on Jung's theories. It was designed to make it possible to determine the dominant functions within the three dimensions described by Jung, namely, **extraversion-introversion**, **sensing-intuition** and **thinking-feeling**. That first test became the inspiration for other researchers. In 1942, again in America, Isabel Briggs Myers and Katherine Briggs began using their own personality test, broadening Gray's and Wheelwright's classic, three-dimensional model to include a fourth: **judging-perceiving**. The majority of subsequent personality typologies and tests drawing on Jung's theories also take that fourth dimension into account. They include the American typology published by David W. Keirsey in 1978 and the personality test developed in the nineteen seventies by Aušra Augustinavičiūtė, a Lithuanian psychologist. Over the following decades, other European researchers followed in their footsteps, creating more four-dimensional personality typologies and tests for use in personal coaching and career counselling.

ID16™© figures among that group. An independent typology developed by Polish educator and manager Jaroslaw Jankowski, it was published in the first decade of the twenty-first century. ID16™© is based on Carl Jung's classic theory and, like other contemporary Jungian typologies, it follows a four-dimensional path, terming those dimensions the **four natural inclinations**. These inclinations are dichotomous in nature and the picture they provide gives us information regarding a person's personality type. Analysis of the first inclination is intended to determine the dominant **source of life energy**, this being either the exterior or the interior world. Analysis of the second inclination defines the dominant **mode of assimilating information**, which occurs via the senses or via intuition. Analysis of the third inclination supplies a description of the **decision-making mode**, where either mind or heart is dominant, while analysis of the fourth inclination produces a definition of the dominant **lifestyle** as either organised or spontaneous. The combination of all these natural inclinations results in **sixteen possible personality types**.

One remarkable feature of the ID16™© typology is its practical dimension. It describes the individual personality types in action – at work, in daily life and in interpersonal relations. It neither concentrates on the internal dynamics of personality nor does it undertake any theoretical attempts at explaining or commenting on invisible, interior processes. The focus is turned more toward the ways in which a given personality type manifests itself externally and how it affects the surrounding world. This emphasis on the social aspect of personality places ID16™© somewhat closer to the previously mentioned typology developed by Aušra Augustinavičiūtė.

Each of the ID16™© personality types is the result of a given person's natural inclinations.

There is nothing evaluative or judgemental about ascribing a person to a given type, though. No particular personality type is 'better' or 'worse' than any other. Each type is quite simply different and each has its own potential strengths and weaknesses. ID16™© makes it possible to identify and describe those differences. It helps us to understand ourselves and discover our place in the world.

Familiarity with our personality profile enables us to make full use of our potential and work on the areas which might cause us trouble. It is an invaluable aid in everyday life, in solving problems, in building healthy relationships with other people and in making decisions relating to our education and careers.

Determining personality is a process which is neither arbitrary nor mechanical in nature. As the 'owner and user' of our personality, each and every one of us is fully capable of defining which type we belong to. The individual's role is thus pivotal. This self-identification can be achieved either by analysing the descriptions of the ID16™© personality types and steadily narrowing down the fields of choice or by taking the short cut provided by the ID16™© Personality Test.[1] The role played by each 'personality user' is equally crucial when it comes to the test, given that the outcome depends entirely on the answers they provide.

---

[1] The test can be found in *Why Are We So Different? Your Guide to the 16 Personality Types* by Jaroslaw Jankowski.

Identifying personality types helps us to know both ourselves and others. Nonetheless, it should not be treated as some kind of future-determining oracle. No personality type can ever justify our weaknesses or poor interpersonal relationships. It might, however, help us to understand their causes!

ID16™© treats personality type not as a static, genetic, pre-determined condition, but as a product of innate and acquired characteristics. As such, it is a concept which neither diminishes free will nor engages in pigeonholing people. What it does is open up new perspectives for us, encouraging us to work on ourselves and indicating the areas where that work is most needed.

The Administrator (ESTJ)

THE ID16™© PERSONALITY TYPOLOGY

The Personality in a Nutshell

Life motto: We'll get the job done!

In brief, administrators …

are hard-working, responsible and extremely loyal. Energetic and decisive, they value order, stability, security and clear rules. They are matter-of-fact and businesslike, logical, rational and practical and possess the capability to assimilate large amounts of detailed information.

Superb organisers, they are intolerant of ineffectuality, wastefulness and slothfulness. True to their convictions and direct in their contact with others, they present their point of view decisively and openly express critical opinions, sometimes hurting other people as a result.

The *administrator*'s four natural inclinations:

- source of life energy: the exterior world
- mode of assimilating information: via the senses
- decision-making mode: the mind
- lifestyle: organised

Similar personality types:

- the Animator
- the Inspector
- the Practitioner

Statistical data:

- *administrators* constitute between ten and thirteen per cent of the global community
- men predominate among *administrators* (60 per cent)
- the United States is an example of a nation corresponding to the *administrator's* profile[2]

The Four-Letter Code

In terms of Jungian personality typology, the universal four-letter code for the *administrator* is ESTJ.

---

[2] What this means is not that all the residents of the USA fall within this personality type, but that American society as a whole possesses a great many of the character traits typical of the *administrator*.

General character traits

Administrators are decisive, self-confident and brimming with energy. They are extraordinarily true to their convictions and have a common-sense attitude to life. They do not concern themselves with abstract theories, conjectures and digressions. What interests them is the nitty-gritty: facts, figures and evidence.

Perception and thinking

Administrators unceasingly monitor the world around them, seeking out manifestations of ineffectiveness and wastefulness. An awareness of any potential for improvement spurs them into action. It is normally difficult to involve them in an activity which produces anything other than concrete solutions to tangible problems. They generally have a sceptical attitude towards new concepts and speculations on matters of potential possibilities or theories which have no practical application. They have no fondness for experiments, preferring tried and tested methods of action. If they have to make a decision about the future, they most often do so on the basis of either their own previous experience or that of others.

When preparing to get involved in something, they usually begin by studying the situation thoroughly and devote considerable time to gathering the relevant data. They work to obtain as much information as possible in order to select the best option.

Administrators express their opinions openly. If they dislike something, they will say so. As a rule, they are convinced that they are in the right. Because they assume that what other people have to offer them is negligible, they set little store by their opinions and viewpoints.

As others see them

Other people perceive *administrators* as industrious, hard-working and responsible. However, their directness, self-assurance and condescending manner often intimidate or irritate others. They are frequently considered to be people who 'always know best'. Some also give the impression of being rather inflexible, overly formal, inordinately organised and 'too fussy by half'.

In turn, what irritates *administrators* in others is incompetence, carelessness, thoughtlessness and recklessness. They are incapable of understanding people who are notoriously unpunctual, fail to keep their word, spend money rashly or have no respect for time, be it their own or other people's. They have no liking for those who flout widely recognised principles, take short cuts or think only of themselves. People who, despite their lack of experience, believe themselves to be outstanding experts are another source of annoyance to them.

Life compass

Administrators value tradition, widely accepted standards and time-honoured rules of behaviour. They are extraordinarily true to their convictions and behave in accordance with the principles they hold dear. In general, they have an enormous respect for authority and are good citizens, being responsible and dutiful. They wish to make a practical contribution to the proper functioning of state and local community alike. They value stability, security and predictability and have zero tolerance for behaviour which disrupts the harmony of the social order and represents a threat to it. Radicalism and extremism affront them.

They also dislike outlandishness and any kind of deviation from the widely accepted norms of behaviour. Their attitude towards changes, new concepts and experiments is cautious. While not opposed to them, they do want to be certain that the results will be practical and beneficial, for instance by giving rise to increased productivity or greater economisation. They adhere to the 'if it ain't broke, don't fix it' philosophy and thus dislike the 'change for change's sake' approach.

Organisational modes

Administrators need structures. They cannot abide muddle, chaos and improvisation. They like things to be orderly and well-organised and are incapable of functioning in an environment which lacks rules and norms. When they can see the potential for streamlining a system, improving its effectiveness and efficiency or putting a stop to waste, they feel stirred to take action. They readily take on the responsibility of solving an existing problem and are natural leaders.

With their ability to create plans of action and determine procedures and their competence in organising the work of others, they are outstanding administrators … hence the name for this personality type. They like to have control over a situation. To some people, this appears to spring from a desire for power or authority; however, in that, they are mistaken. In fact, it follows from the *administrator's* conviction that a task will only be done properly if he or she supervises everything in person. In general, *administrators* are extremely demanding, of themselves just as much as of others, as well as being highly critical. They hold no brief for laziness, unreliability and neglect of responsibilities and duties. Incapable of standing passively by and observing injustices in the making or idly watching as the rules they believe in are broken, they are ever ready to voice their opposition, even though it may cost them dear.

By nature responsible, practical and punctual, they expect the same of others. They strive to carry out the duties and responsibilities entrusted to them to the very best of their ability. Their preference is for operating according to plan, which is why they usually map out what they intend to do in advance and will often draw up their schedule for the day, either in their minds or on paper, or make a 'to-do' list. As a rule, they adhere to accepted procedures conscientiously and are happy to submit to those in authority, believing this to be indispensable to operating effectively. They are able to spot occurrences of ineffectiveness which have gone unnoticed by others and they set great store by time, doing their utmost to make optimum use of it.

Leisure

Administrators enjoy the simple things in life: spending time with those closest to them, sharing meals, having fun and playing games together. They are capable of relaxing and unwinding, though not when an unfinished task awaits them! In general, they like active leisure pursuits. Prolonged periods of stress cause them to feel alienated and superfluous and they begin to doubt their own worth. At times, tension and friction can lead them to become either withdrawn or dogmatic and stubborn.

Socially

Administrators enjoy being among people and get on well with new faces. Though often formal in their contact with others, they have no problem in establishing relationships with them and are also easy to get to know. They try to be tactful and courteous, but will not allow themselves to be used and never seek other people's sympathy, not at any price. Subjected to pressure and manipulation, they remain unreceptive and unyielding.

As a rule, they have a need to be affiliated to a larger group, often becoming involved in social activities and belonging to all sorts of clubs, associations and communities. Shunning responsibilities would be alien to them and they readily devote their time to accomplishing the aims they identify with. They also set great store by family customs and celebrations, as well as nurturing their relationships with their friends, seizing every possible opportunity of meeting up with them.

Administrators are exceptionally loyal to those close to them Responsibility and duty are the foundations of their creed as far as interpersonal relationships are concerned. They give of themselves unstintingly and expect the same of others. Always ready to come to other people's aid, they are unfailingly generous with their time and energy when it comes to extending a helping hand, providing those who need it with support, infusing them with faith in themselves and assisting them in discovering their talents. They are also unsparing in sharing their own experience.

They are happy when others perceive their dedication and show their thanks. As believers in the maxim that actions speak louder than words, their way of expressing affection and devotion is practical. They rarely show their emotions and are rather scant in their praise. Their inability to read the emotions and feelings of others is also a problem for them; with their direct pronouncements and crisp, explicit comments, there are times when they unwittingly hurt people's feelings.

Amongst friends

Administrators will usually surround themselves with people they can both trust and count on without fail, deriving real joy from spending time with them. Strangers will often perceive *administrators* as formal and strict traditionalists. Their friends, though, know that there is another side to their character and that they are quite capable of having a good time, joking around and being the centre of attention. Although their direct style sometimes intimidates people, it also makes them easy to get to know, since they speak their minds and make no secret of their opinions and points of view. Amongst friends, they neither try to play any kind of role nor to adopt a mask of any sort.

Administrators often make friendships which last a lifetime. As a rule, they integrate rapidly with their colleagues, not only enjoying work-related gatherings and ice-breaking events, but also meeting up outside the workplace. They hold experienced, competent and influential people in esteem and have no liking for those who are flamboyant or eccentric or who go against convention. Finding a common language with people who perceive the world in a wholly different way from theirs is also difficult for them. They most often strike up friendships with *animators, inspectors* and *directors* and most rarely with *idealists*, *enthusiasts*, *counsellors* and other *administrators*. Their friends and acquaintances value their devotion and reliability, though at times, despite having known them for a long time, they feel overwhelmed by their self-assurance.

As life partners

To *administrators*, life partnerships are sacred. In general, they give no house room to thoughts of divorce, although if their relationship does collapse, they are able to pick themselves up and move on quite quickly. Family is one of the most important things in their lives and they consider every kind of familial obligation to be of the utmost importance. They are a rock for their nearest and dearest and are always willing to help them out. They consider providing for their family and assuring their security to be their personal responsibility; those closest to them warrant their utmost endeavour and devotion. They show their attachments and dedication in practical ways, involving themselves in family life and fulfilling their duties and obligations.

In taking on responsibility for their nearest and dearest, they will sometimes attempt to instruct and advise them, an approach which generally fails to go down too well with their partners. Neither are they capable of reading and interpreting their partner's feelings and emotions and, as a result, they will sometimes unwittingly hurt them with their blunt comments or remarks. Rarely will an *administrator* show them warmth, and, as a rule, they are unlikely to shower them with compliments either, more often praising them for a concrete achievement. Their partner might therefore be left with a sense that their emotional needs are somehow unfulfilled.

The natural candidates for an *administrator's* life partner are people of a personality type akin to their own: *animators*, *inspectors* or *practitioners*. Building mutual understanding and harmonious relations will be easier in a union of that kind. Nonetheless, experience has taught us that people are also capable of creating happy and successful relationships despite what would seem to be an evident typological incompatibility. Moreover, the differences between two partners can lend added dynamics to a relationship and engender personal development. Indeed, for many people, this is a prospect that appears more attractive than the vision of a harmonious relationship wherein concord and full, mutual understanding hold sway.

As parents

Administrators take their parental responsibilities extremely seriously. The role of parent comes naturally to them and they invest every effort in bringing their children up to be responsible and independent people. They prefer the traditional model of the family, where the parents represent figures of authority to their children and warrant respect; 'palling around with the kids' is out of the question. Disobedience and the breaking of established rules are not tolerated and they are demanding and capable of applying discipline.

Unstinting in their criticism, *administrators* are also sparing when it comes to praising their children. They are often unperceptive of their emotional needs and fail to demonstrate a sufficient amount of warmth. On the other hand, they are eager to teach them decent behaviour and help them to distinguish between right and wrong, as well as instilling them with a practical, logical and common-sense approach to problems. They will show their impatience when their children continually make the same mistakes or blatantly disregard their duties and obligations. Yet they are highly devoted to their offspring and unstinting in giving them their time and energy. Later in life, their children appreciate them first and foremost for their ready dedication, for being their support and for inculcating them with the rules that make the world go round.

Work and career paths

Administrators are titans at work and engage to the full in accomplishing the tasks entrusted to them. They are incapable of working to less than their maximum potential. They cope superbly with practical tasks and are able to comply with complex procedures and conform with top-down guidelines and instructions. Their preference is for stable surroundings and they have no liking for frequent change.

As part of a team

Administrators believe that it is only by carrying out one's duties conscientiously, collaborating and sticking to the established rules that a given goal can be achieved. They make for trouble-free subordinates who can be relied on and are capable of working harmoniously with others. It is rare for them to question the instructions of those in charge or ignore the requisite procedures.

Organisation at work

Administrators need no reminders, urging, supervision or checking up on, since they are self-motivating and derive great pleasure from a job well done.

They are ideally suited to tasks demanding organisational skills and a love of orderliness. They are unrivalled when it comes to drawing up all kinds of plans of actions, schedules, systems, charts, diagrams and other graphic representations, to say nothing of putting them into practice. When they are charged with managing a team of employees or a system, then rest assured! The requisite procedures will be observed, the deadlines will be met and the job will be done effectively, efficiently and without disruptions.

Administrators have no understanding of people who fail to apply themselves to the tasks entrusted to them or to follow through on earlier undertakings or who consciously disregard regulations. They feel a sense of injustice when reliable employees are treated the same as those whose approach to their duties lacks diligence. They are definite supporters of remuneration on the basis of achievement and, in their view, 'fair' is not in the least synonymous with 'equal'.

Tasks

Administrators prefer practical tasks with a short time span. They enjoy solving tangible and concrete problems and like their work to have visible results. It gives them enormous satisfaction to see a system which was previously defective begin to function efficiently or resources which were being wasted now being put to more effective use or newly organised working procedures and practices giving rise to measurable savings of time. They cope less well in situations which demand thinking ahead into the future, reference to theory, improvisation or relying on intuition.

Companies and institutions

Administrators like the people in charge to respect their subordinates, value their experience and reward their achievements. Given their reliability, loyalty and predictability, they have a predisposition for jobs in administrative fields, both in state institutions and businesses. They enjoy the stability and prestige which goes hand in hand with working in large public organisations or enterprises with an established position. As employees, they are extremely loyal and fit in well in hierarchies and corporate structures providing the possibility of promotion. They will often spend the best part of their lives with one employer, steadily climbing the career ladder and, quite often, making their way to the very top. They also cope well with competition and rivalry.

In positions of authority

Administrators have a natural talent for leadership and are capable of organising and supervising the work of others. They enjoy making decisions, influencing the course of events and getting involved in settling practical problems. They are less good at coping with issues of a theoretical nature and strategic planning.

As leaders, they will more often perform the role of manager than of visionary and their preferred style for dealing with their subordinates is official and formal. While they are normally critical and demanding in their appraisals, they are also unusually objective and fair. They fix priorities and set clear goals, making it easy for them to evaluate the achievements of the employees they supervise. In general, they tend to be impatient, wanting to see tasks which are waiting to be carried out accomplished as soon as possible. Knowing that there is work outstanding or that a job may not be done on time causes them a definite sense of unease.

In focusing on urgent jobs, they often lose sight of crucial tasks, particularly when a longer time span is involved. They can also become overburdened with duties, since they have a problematic tendency to exercise excessive supervision over their subordinates and may thus fail to delegate sufficiently. This springs from their conviction that they will do the job quicker and better themselves, which is, indeed, very often the case. However, this *modus operandi* discourages those they supervise from working independently and deprives them of the privilege of learning from their mistakes.

Professions

Knowledge of our own personality profile and natural preferences provides us with invaluable help in choosing the optimal path in our professional careers. Experience has shown that, while *administrators* are perfectly able to work and find fulfilment in a range of fields, their personality type naturally predisposes them to the following professions and fields:

- administrator
- auditor
- banking

- bookkeeper
- chef
- clerk
- detective
- director
- economist
- engineer
- office manager
- inspector
- insurance agent
- IT
- judge
- lawyer
- librarian
- manager
- pharmacist
- police officer
- politician
- project coordinator
- public administration
- referee/umpire
- sales representative
- scholar
- soldier
- sports coach
- teacher
- technician
- tertiary educator

Potential strengths and weaknesses

Like any other personality type, *administrators* have their potential strengths and weaknesses and this potential can be cultivated in a variety of ways. Their personal happiness and professional fulfilment depend on whether they make the most of the 'pluses' offered by their personality type and face up to its inherent dangers. Here, then, is a SUMMARY of those 'pluses' and dangers:

Potential strengths

Administrators are enthusiastic, friendly and ready to extend a helping hand to others. In terms of their work, they are self-motivating and have a sense of duty. Energetic, decisive and matter-of-fact, they are happy to accept responsibility for accomplishing tasks. With their natural leadership skills, they are capable of heading up teams and supervising others. They are able to evaluate impartially and objectively and are logical, rational and practical. They will always speak their mind and are direct in their contact with others, accept criticism well and are also capable of carrying out critical appraisals.

As a rule, they are highly perceptive, have good memories and are able to assimilate large amounts of detailed information. When they can see the potential for streamlining a system, improving its effectiveness and efficiency or putting a stop to waste, they feel stirred to take action. Capable when it comes to drawing up plans and establishing procedures, they will spot flaws and shortcomings imperceptible to others. They are hard-working, responsible and extremely loyal and complete the jobs they are given on time or, indeed, quite often before the deadline. They are incapable of consciously working to less than their full potential. With their love of order and organisational flair, they are excellent and capable resource managers and superb system organisers and administrators. Characterised by their independence and resistance to manipulation, they are true to their convictions and, no matter what the prevailing opinion might be, they stick to their own principles.

Potential weaknesses

As a rule, *administrators* assume that they are right. They will often shut out points of view which differ from their own, and as a result they narrow their own field of perception. With their natural inclination to instruct and advise, they will sometimes behave condescendingly and try to exert pressure on others. They have a tendency to focus excessively on details, which often means that they fail to perceive the bigger picture. Digesting theories and predicting the future consequences of present decisions and events comes hard to them. They feel that they are on very uncertain ground in situations which demand that they think ahead into the future or rely on intuition or improvisation. They have an inclination to concentrate on urgent tasks at the expense of important ones. Two problems that frequently crop up are their failure to delegate sufficiently and their habit of interfering in the work of their subordinates or colleagues. They are highly demanding, their expectations can be unrealistic and they can give the impression of being almost impossible to satisfy.

Reading the emotions and feelings of others is difficult for them, which often means that they unwittingly upset people. They have little awareness of the fact that their bluntly expressed opinions and jokes might be hurtful to others. Their mode of communication may not always be appropriate to the situation and circumstances in which they find themselves. Expressing their own emotions and demonstrating warmth towards others is also hard for them. In general, they are sparing in their praise and generous with their criticism. Being somewhat inflexible by nature, they find it difficult to cope with change. They can be stubborn, dogmatic, impatient and irritable and may be overly focused on immediate benefits, social status and material possessions.

Personal development

Administrators' personal development depends on the extent to which they make use of their natural potential and surmount the dangers inherent in their personality type. What follows are some practical tips which, together, form a specific guide that we might call *The Administrator's Ten Commandments*.

Be more understanding

Show more patience towards children, young people and those who have less experience or are less able. Not everyone is skilled in the same fields.

If others are unable to cope with a task, this is not always a sign of their ill will or laziness.

Listen

Demonstrate an interest in others, even when you disagree with them or are convinced that they are wrong. Save your response until you have heard them out. The ability to listen could well revolutionise your relationship with others!

Accept change

When you look at ideas which might bring about change or undermine the current order and discard them in advance, you are throwing away the opportunity for development and depriving yourself of countless valuable experiences. Change always brings risk, but it will usually be rather less than you expected.

Admit that you can make mistakes

Always being right is neither obligatory nor likely. Sometimes you might be mistaken. At times, reality is more complex than you thought and both sides may be right, at any rate partially. Avoid assuming that no one else knows about a given matter as well as you do; this, in itself, is a mistake!

Praise others

Make the most of every occasion to appreciate other people, say something nice to them and praise them for something they have done. At work, value people not only for the job they do, but also for who they are. Then wait and see. The difference will come as a pleasant surprise!

Criticise less

Not everyone has your ability to handle constructive criticism. In many cases, being openly critical can have a destructive effect. Studies have shown that praising positive behaviour, albeit limited, motivates people more than criticising negative conduct.

Treat others kindly

People have a desire to be seen as something more than just tools serving to accomplish a goal. They long for their emotions, feelings and enthusiasms to be perceived. Mix with people, communicate with them, try to put yourself in their shoes and understand what they are going through, what fascinates them, what worries them, what they fear …

Leave some things to take their natural course

There is no way you can have everything under your personal control and no way you can manage to be in command of absolutely everything. Leave less important matters to take their natural course. Lay less crucial decisions aside. Stop putting all that effort into reforming other people. You will save energy and avoid frustration.

Stop blaming others for your problems

Your problems may not only be caused by others – they might also be caused by you! You, too, are capable of oversights and mistakes. You, too, can be the root of a problem.

Control your emotions

If you feel that you might well explode, then try to relax, wind down and think about something else for a moment. Outbursts of anger help neither you nor the people around you.

Well-known figures

Below is a list of some well-known people who match the *administrator's* profile:

- **Carry Nation** (1846-1911); an American temperance activist.
- **Bette Davis** (Ruth Elizabeth Davis; 1908-1989); an American stage and screen actress whose films include *All About Eve*. The winner of numerous prestigious awards, she is considered one of the greatest actresses of all time.
- **Harry S. Truman** (1884-1972); the 33rd president of the United States.
- **Billy Graham** (William Franklin Graham, Jr; 1918-2018); an American Baptist preacher, one of the most famous evangelists in the world and the author of a number of books, including *Peace with God*.

- **Sandra Day O'Connor** (born in 1930); an American lawyer and the first female judge to be appointed a Justice of the Supreme Court of the United States.
- **George W. Bush** (born in 1946); the 43rd president of the United States.
- **Susan Sarandon** (Susan Abigail Tomalin; born in 1946); an American screen actress whose films include *Dead Man Walking*.
- **John de Lancie** (born in 1948); an American screen actor whose films include *Star Trek*.
- **Bruce Willis** (born in 1955); an American screen actor whose films include *Armageddon*, he is also a singer.
- **Mickey Rourke** (born in 1956); an American screen actor whose films include *Animal Factory*, he is also a screenwriter.
- **Laura Linney** (born in 1964); an American screen actress whose films include *Mystic River*.
- **Brendan Fraser** (born in 1968); an American-Canadian screen actor whose films include *The Mummy*.
- **Daniel Craig** (born in 1968); an English stage and screen actor who took on the role of James Bond in 2005. His first Bond movie was *Casino Royale*.

The ID16™© Personality Types in a Nutshell

The Administrator (ESTJ)

Life motto: We'll get the job done!

Administrators are hard-working, responsible and extremely loyal. Energetic and decisive, they value order, stability, security and clear rules. They are matter-of-fact and businesslike, logical, rational and practical and possess the capability to assimilate large amounts of detailed information.

Superb organisers, they are intolerant of ineffectuality, wastefulness and slothfulness. True to their convictions and direct in their contact with others, they present their point of view decisively and openly express critical opinions, sometimes hurting other people as a result.

The *administrator*'s four natural inclinations:

- source of life energy: the exterior world
- mode of assimilating information: via the senses
- decision-making mode: the mind
- lifestyle: organised

Similar personality types:

- the Animator
- the Inspector
- the Practitioner

Statistical data:

- *administrators* constitute between ten and thirteen per cent of the global community
- men predominate among *administrators* (60 per cent)
- the United States is an example of a nation corresponding to the *administrator's* profile[3]

Find out more!

The Administrator. Your Guide to the ESTJ Personality Type by Jaroslaw Jankowski

---

[3] What this means is not that all the residents of the USA fall within this personality type, but that American society as a whole possesses a great many of the character traits typical of the *administrator.*

The Advocate (ESFJ)

Life motto: How can I help you?

Advocates are well-organised, energetic and enthusiastic. Practical, responsible and conscientious, they are sincere and exceptionally gregarious.

Advocates are perceptive of human feelings, emotions and needs. They value harmony and find criticism and conflict difficult to bear. With their sensitivity to any and every manifestation of injustice, prejudice or detriment to another, they are genuinely interested in other people's problems and take real delight in helping them and tending to their needs, while often neglecting their own. They have a tendency to do everything for others and can be vulnerable to manipulation.

The *advocate*'s four natural inclinations:

- source of life energy: the exterior world
- mode of assimilating information: via the senses
- decision-making mode: the heart
- lifestyle: organised

Similar personality types:

- the Presenter
- the Protector
- the Artist

Statistical data:

- *advocates* constitute between ten and thirteen per cent of the global community
- women predominate among *advocates* (70 per cent)
- Canada is an example of a nation corresponding to the *advocate's* profile

Find out more!

The Advocate. Your Guide to the ESFJ Personality Type by Jaroslaw Jankowski

The Animator (ESTP)

Life motto: Let's DO something!

Animators are energetic, active and enterprising. Fond of the company of others, they have the ability to enjoy the moment and are spontaneous, flexible and open to change.

Animators are inspirers and instigators, spurring others to act. Being logical, rational and pragmatic realists, they are wearied by abstract concepts and solutions for the future. Their focus is on solving concrete problems in the here and now. They have difficulties with organising and planning and can be impulsive, acting first and thinking later.

The *animator's* four natural inclinations:

- source of life energy: the exterior world
- mode of assimilating information: via the senses

- decision-making mode: the mind
- lifestyle: spontaneous

Similar personality types:

- the Administrator
- the Practitioner
- the Inspector

Statistical data:

- *animators* constitute between six and ten per cent of the global community
- men predominate among *animators* (60 per cent)
- Australia is an example of a nation corresponding to the *animator's* profile

Find out more!

The Animator. Your Guide to the ESTP Personality Type by Jaroslaw Jankowski

The Artist (ISFP)

Life motto: Let's create something!

Artists are sensitive, creative and original, with a sense of the aesthetic and natural artistic talents. Independent in character, they follow their own system of values and are optimistic in outlook, with a positive approach to life and an ability to enjoy the moment.

Helping others is a source of joy to them. They find abstract theories tedious and would rather create reality than talk about it, although starting on something new comes more easily to them than finishing what they have already started. They have difficulty in voicing their own desires and needs.

The *artist's* four natural inclinations:

- source of life energy: the interior world
- mode of assimilating information: via the senses
- decision-making mode: the heart
- lifestyle: spontaneous

Similar personality types:

- the Protector
- the Presenter
- the Advocate

Statistical data:

- *artists* constitute between six and nine per cent of the global community
- women predominate among *artists* (60 per cent)
- China is an example of a nation corresponding to the *artist's* profile

Find out more!

The Artist. Your Guide to the ISFP Personality Type by Jaroslaw Jankowski

The Counsellor (ENFJ)

Life motto: My friends are my world

Counsellors are optimistic, enthusiastic and quick-witted. Courteous and tactful, they have an extraordinary gift for empathy and find joy in acting for the good of others, with no thought of themselves. They have the ability to influence other people, inspiring them, eliciting their hidden potential and giving them faith in their own powers. Radiating warmth, they draw others to them and often help them in solving their personal problems.

Counsellors can be over-trusting and have a tendency to view the world through rose-tinted glasses. With their focus on other people, they often forget about their own needs.

The *counsellor's* four natural inclinations:

- source of life energy: the exterior world
- mode of assimilating information: intuition
- decision-making mode: the heart
- lifestyle: organised

Similar personality types:

- the Enthusiast
- the Mentor
- the Idealist

Statistical data:

- *counsellors* constitute between three and five per cent of the global community
- women predominate among *counsellors* (80 per cent)
- France is an example of a nation corresponding to the *counsellor's* profile

Find out more!

The Counsellor. Your Guide to the ENFJ Personality Type by Jaroslaw Jankowski

The Director (ENTJ)

Life motto: I'll tell you what you need to do.

Directors are independent, active and decisive. Rational, logical and creative, when they analyse problems they look at the wider picture and are able to foresee the future consequences of human activities. They are characterised by optimism and a healthy sense of their own worth and are capable of transforming theoretical concepts into concrete, practical plans of action.

Visionaries, mentors and organisers, *directors* possess natural leadership skills. Their powerful personalities and direct and critical style can often have an intimidating effect, causing them problems in their interpersonal relationships.

The *director's* four natural inclinations:

- source of life energy: the exterior world

- mode of assimilating information: intuition
- decision-making mode: the mind
- lifestyle: organised

Similar personality types:

- the Innovator
- the Strategist
- the Logician

Statistical data:

- *directors* constitute between two and five per cent of the global community
- men predominate among *directors* (70 per cent)
- Holland is an example of a nation corresponding to the *director's* profile

Find out more!

The Director. Your Guide to the ENTJ Personality Type by Jaroslaw Jankowski

The Enthusiast (ENFP)

Life motto: We'll manage!

Enthusiasts are energetic, enthusiastic and optimistic. Capable of enjoying life and looking ahead to the future, they are dynamic, quick-witted and creative. They have a liking for people in general, value honest and genuine relationships and are warm, sincere and emotional. Criticism is something they handle badly. With their gift for empathy and ability to perceive people's needs, feelings and motives, they both inspire others and infect them with their own enthusiasm.

They love to be at the centre of events and are flexible and capable of improvising. Their inclination leads towards idealistic notions. Being easily distracted, they have problems with seeing things through to the end.

The *enthusiast's* four natural inclinations:

- source of life energy: the exterior world
- mode of assimilating information: intuition
- decision-making mode: the heart
- lifestyle: spontaneous

Similar personality types:

- the Counsellor
- the Idealist
- the Mentor

Statistical data:

- *enthusiasts* constitute between five and eight per cent of the global community
- women predominate among *enthusiasts* (60 per cent)
- Italy is an example of a nation corresponding to the *enthusiast's* profile

Find out more!

The Enthusiast. Your Guide to the ENFP Personality Type by Jaroslaw Jankowski

The Idealist (INFP)

Life motto: We CAN live differently.

Idealists are sensitive, loyal, and creative. Living in accordance with the values they hold is of immense importance to them and they both manifest an interest in the reality of the spirit and delve deeply into the mysteries of life. Wrapped up in the world's problems and open to the needs of other people, they prize harmony and balance.

Idealists are romantic; not only are they able to show love, but they also need warmth and affection themselves. With their outstanding ability to read other people's feelings and emotions, they build healthy, profound and enduring relationships. They feel that they are on very shaky ground in situations of conflict and have no real resistance to stress and criticism.

The *idealist's* four natural inclinations:

- source of life energy: the interior world
- mode of assimilating information: intuition
- decision-making mode: the heart
- lifestyle: spontaneous

Similar personality types:

- the Mentor
- the Enthusiast
- the Counsellor

Statistical data:

- *idealists* constitute between one and four per cent of the global community
- women predominate among *idealists* (60 per cent)
- Thailand is an example of a nation corresponding to the *idealist's* profile

Find out more!

The Idealist. Your Guide to the INFP Personality Type by Jaroslaw Jankowski

The Innovator (ENTP)

Life motto: How about trying a different approach…?

Innovators are inventive, original and independent. Optimistic, energetic and enterprising, they are people of action who love being at the centre of events and solving 'insoluble' problems. Their thoughts are turned to the future and they are curious about the world and visionary by nature. Open to new concepts and ideas, they enjoy new experiences and experiments and have the ability to identify the connections between separate events.

Innovators are spontaneous, communicative and self-assured. However, they tend to overestimate their own possibilities and have problems with seeing things through to the end. They are also inclined to be impatient and to take risks.

The *innovator's* four natural inclinations:

- source of life energy: the exterior world
- mode of assimilating information: intuition
- decision-making mode: the mind
- lifestyle: spontaneous

Similar personality types:

- the Director
- the Logician
- the Strategist

Statistical data:

- *innovators* constitute between three and five per cent of the global community
- men predominate among *innovators* (70 per cent)
- Israel is an example of a nation corresponding to the *innovator's* profile

Find out more!

The Innovator. Your Guide to the ENTP Personality Type by Jaroslaw Jankowski

The Inspector (ISTJ)

Life motto: *Duty first.*

Inspectors are people who can always be counted on. Well-mannered, punctual, reliable, conscientious and responsible, when they give their word, they keep it. Being analytical, methodical, systematic and logical by nature, they tend be seen as serious, cold and reserved. They prize calm, stability and order, have no fondness for change and like clear principles and concrete rules.

Inspectors are hard-working, persevering and capable of seeing things through to the end. As perfectionists, they try to exercise control over everything within their sphere and are sparing in their praise. They also underrate the importance of other people's feelings and emotions.

The *inspector's* four natural inclinations:

- source of life energy: the interior world
- mode of assimilating information: via the senses
- decision-making mode: the mind
- lifestyle: organised

Similar personality types:

- the Practitioner
- the Administrator
- the Animator

Statistical data:

- *inspectors* constitute between six and ten per cent of the global community
- men predominate among *inspectors* (60 per cent)
- Switzerland is an example of a nation corresponding to the *inspector's* profile

Find out more!

The Inspector. Your Guide to the ISTJ Personality Type by Jaroslaw Jankowski

The Logician (INTP)

Life motto: Above all else, seek to discover the truths about the world.

Logicians are original, resourceful and creative. With a love for solving problems of a theoretical nature, they are analytical, quick-witted, enthusiastically disposed towards new concepts and have the ability to connect individual phenomena, educing general rules and theories from them. Logical, exact and inquiring, they are quick to spot incoherence and inconsistency.

Logicians are independent, sceptical of existing solutions and authorities, tolerant and open to new challenges. When immersed in thought, they will sometimes lose touch with the outside world.

The *logician's* four natural inclinations:

- source of life energy: the interior world

- mode of assimilating information: intuition
- decision-making mode: the mind
- lifestyle: spontaneous

Similar personality types:

- the Strategist
- the Innovator
- the Director

Statistical data:

- *logicians* constitute between two and three per cent of the global community;
- men predominate among *logicians* (80 per cent)
- India is an example of a nation corresponding to the *logician's* profile

Find out more!

The Logician. Your Guide to the INTP Personality Type by Jaroslaw Jankowski

The Mentor (INFJ)

Life motto: The world CAN be a better place!

Mentors are creative and sensitive. With their gaze fixed firmly on the future, they spot opportunities and potential imperceptible to others. Idealists and visionaries, they are geared towards helping people and are conscientious, responsible and, at one and the same time, courteous, caring and friendly. They strive to understand the mechanisms governing the world and view problems from a wide perspective.

Superb listeners and observers, *mentors* are characterised by their extraordinary empathy, intuition and trust of people and are capable of reading the feelings and emotions of others. They find criticism and conflict difficult to bear and can come across as enigmatic.

The *mentor's* four natural inclinations:

- source of life energy: the interior world
- mode of assimilating information: intuition
- decision-making mode: the heart
- lifestyle: organised

Similar personality types:

- the Idealist
- the Counsellor
- the Enthusiast

Statistical data:

- *mentors* constitute one per cent of the global community and are the most rarely occurring of the sixteen personality types
- women predominate among *mentors* (80 per cent)
- Norway is an example of a nation corresponding to the *mentor's* profile

Find out more!

The Mentor. Your Guide to the INFJ Personality Type by Jaroslaw Jankowski

The Practitioner (ISTP)

Life motto: Actions speak louder than words.

Practitioners are optimistic and spontaneous, with a positive approach to life. Reserved and independent, they hold true to their personal convictions and view external principles and norms with scepticism. They find abstract concepts and solutions for the future tiresome and would far rather roll up their sleeves and get to work on solving tangible and concrete problems.

Adapting well to new places and situations, they enjoy fresh challenges and risks and are capable of keeping a cool head in the face of threats and danger. Their general reticence and extreme reserve when it comes to expressing their opinions mean that other people may often find them impenetrable.

The *practitioner's* four natural inclinations:

- source of life energy: the interior world
- mode of assimilating information: via the senses
- decision-making mode: the mind
- lifestyle: spontaneous

Similar personality types:

- the Inspector
- the Animator
- the Administrator

Statistical data:

- *practitioners* constitute between six and nine per cent of the global community
- men predominate among *practitioners* (60 per cent)
- Singapore is an example of a nation corresponding to the *practitioner's* profile

Find out more!

The Practitioner. Your Guide to the ISTP Personality Type by Jaroslaw Jankowski

The Presenter (ESFP)

Life motto: Now is the perfect moment!

Presenters are optimistic, energetic and outgoing, with the ability to enjoy life and have fun to the full. Practical, flexible and spontaneous at one and the same time, they enjoy change and new experiences, coping badly with solitude, stagnation and routine.

With their liking for being at the centre of attention, they are natural-born actors and their speaking abilities arouse the interest and enthusiasm of their listeners. Focused as they are on the present moment, they will sometimes lose sight of their long-term aims and can also have problems with foreseeing the consequences of their actions.

The *presenter's* four natural inclinations:

- source of life energy: the exterior world
- mode of assimilating information: via the senses
- decision-making mode: the heart
- lifestyle: spontaneous

Similar personality types:

- the Advocate
- the Artist
- the Protector

Statistical data:

- *presenters* constitute between eight and thirteen per cent of the global community
- women predominate among *presenters* (60 per cent)
- Brazil is an example of a nation corresponding to the *presenter's* profile

Find out more!

The Presenter. Your Guide to the ESFP Personality Type by Jaroslaw Jankowski

The Protector (ISFJ)

Life motto: Your happiness matters to me.

Protectors are sincere, warm-hearted, unassuming, trustworthy and extraordinarily loyal. With their ability to perceive people's needs and their desire to help them, they will always put others first. Practical, well-organised and gifted with both an eye and a memory for detail, they are responsible, hard-working, patient, persevering and capable of seeing things through to the end.

Protectors set great store by tranquillity, stability and friendly relations with others and are skilled at building bridges between people. By the same token, they find conflict and criticism difficult to bear. Given their powerful sense of duty and their constant readiness to come to the aid of others, they can end up being used by people.

The *protector's* four natural inclinations:

- source of life energy: the interior world
- mode of assimilating information: via the senses
- decision-making mode: the heart
- lifestyle: organised

Similar personality types:

- the Artist
- the Advocate
- the Presenter

Statistical data:

- *protectors* constitute between eight and twelve per cent of the global population
- women predominate among *protectors* (70 per cent)
- Sweden is an example of a nation corresponding to the *protector's* profile

Find out more!

The Protector. Your Guide to the ISFJ Personality Type by Jaroslaw Jankowski

The Strategist (INTJ)

Life motto: I can certainly improve this.

Strategists are independent and outstandingly individualistic, with an immense seam of inner energy. Creative, inventive and resourceful, others perceive them as competent, self-assured and, at one and the same time, distant and enigmatic. No matter what they turn their attention to, they will always look at the bigger picture and they have a driving urge to improve the world around them and set it in order.

Well-organised, responsible, critical and demanding, they are difficult to knock off balance – and just as hard to please to the full. Reading the emotions and feelings of others is something they find very problematic.

The *strategist's* four natural inclinations:

- source of life energy: the interior world
- mode of assimilating information: intuition
- decision-making mode: the mind
- lifestyle: organised

Similar personality types:

- the Logician
- the Director
- the Innovator

Statistical data:

- *strategists* constitute between one and two per cent of the global community
- men predominate among *strategists* (80 per cent)
- Finland is an example of a nation corresponding to the *strategist's* profile

Find out more!

The Strategist. Your Guide to the INTJ Personality Type by Jaroslaw Jankowski

Additional information

The four natural inclinations

1. THE DOMINANT SOURCE OF LIFE
   ENERGY

   a. THE EXTERIOR WORLD
      People who draw their energy
      from outside. They need activity
      and contact with others and find
      being alone for any length of time
      hard to bear.

   b. THE INTERIOR WORLD
      People who draw their energy
      from their inner world. They need
      quiet and solitude and feel drained

when they spend any length of time in a group.

2. THE DOMINANT MODE OF ASSIMILATING INFORMATION

    a. VIA THE SENSES
People who rely on the five senses and are persuaded by facts and evidence. They have a liking for methods and practices which are tried and tested and prefer concrete tasks and are realists who trust in experience.

    b. VIA INTUITION
People who rely on the sixth sense and are driven by what they 'feel in their bones'. They have a liking for innovative solutions and problems of a theoretical nature and are characterised by a creative approach to their tasks and the ability to predict.

3. THE DOMINANT DECISION-MAKING MODE

    a. THE MIND
People who are guided by logic and objective principles. They are critical and direct in expressing their opinions.

b. THE HEART
People who are guided by their feelings and values. They long for harmony and mutual understanding with others.

4. THE DOMINANT LIFESTYLE

a. ORGANISED
People who are conscientious and organised. They value order and like to operate according to plan.

b. SPONTANEOUS
People who are spontaneous and value freedom of action. They live for the moment and have no trouble finding their feet in new situations.

The approximate percentage of each personality type in the world population

Personality Type:	Proportion:
• The Administrator (ESTJ):	10-13%
• The Advocate (ESFJ):	10-13%
• The Animator (ESTP):	6-10%
• The Artist (ISFP):	6-9%
• The Counsellor (ENFJ):	3-5 %
• The Director (ENTJ):	2-5%

- The Enthusiast (ENFP):   5-8%
- The Idealist (INFP):   1-4%
- The Innovator (ENTP):   3-5%
- The Inspector (ISTJ):   6-10%
- The Logician (INTP):   2-3%
- The Mentor (INFJ):   ca. 1%
- The Practitioner (ISTP):   6-9%
- The Presenter (ESFP):   8-13%
- The Protector (ISFJ):   8-12%
- The Strategist (INTJ):   1-2%

The approximate percentage of women and men of each personality type in the world population

Personality Type: **Women / Men:**

- The Administrator (ESTJ):   40% / 60%
- The Advocate (ESFJ):   70% / 30%
- The Animator (ESTP):   40% / 60%
- The Artist (ISFP):   60% / 40%
- The Counsellor (ENFJ):   80% / 20%
- The Director (ENTJ):   30% / 70%
- The Enthusiast (ENFP):   60% / 40%
- The Idealist (INFP):   60% / 40%
- The Innovator (ENTP):   30% / 70%
- The Inspector (ISTJ):   40% / 60%
- The Logician (INTP):   20% / 80%
- The Mentor (INFJ):   80% / 20%
- The Practitioner (ISTP):   40% / 60%
- The Presenter (ESFP):   60% / 40%

- The Protector (ISFJ):   70% / 30%
- The Strategist (INTJ):   20% / 80%

Bibliography

- Arraj, Tyra & Arraj, James: *Tracking the Elusive Human, Volume 1: A Practical Guide to C.G. Jung's Psychological Types, W.H. Sheldon's Body and Temperament Types and Their Integration*, Inner Growth Books, 1988
- Arraj, James: *Tracking the Elusive Human, Volume 2: An Advanced Guide to the Typological Worlds of C. G. Jung, W.H. Sheldon, Their Integration, and the Biochemical Typology of the Future*, Inner Growth Books, 1990
- Berens, Linda V.; Cooper, Sue A.; Ernst, Linda K.; Martin, Charles R.; Myers, Steve; Nardi, Dario; Pearman, Roger R.; Segal, Marci; Smith, Melissa: *A Quick Guide to the 16 Personality Types in Organizations: Understanding Personality Differences in the Workplace*, Telos Publications, 2002

- Geier, John G. & Downey, E. Dorothy: *Energetics of Personality*, Aristos Publishing House, 1989

- Hunsaker, Phillip L. & Alessandra, Anthony J.: *The Art of Managing People*, Simon and Schuster, 1986

- Jung, Carl Gustav: *Psychological Types (The Collected Works of C. G. Jung, Vol. 6)*, Princeton University Press, 1976

- Kise, Jane A. G.; Stark, David & Krebs Hirsch, Sandra: *LifeKeys: Discover Who You Are*, Bethany House, 2005

- Kroeger, Otto & Thuesen, Janet: *Type Talk or How to Determine Your Personality Type and Change Your Life*, Delacorte Press, 1988

- Lawrence, Gordon: *People Types and Tiger Stripes*, Center for Applications of Psychological Type, 1993

- Lawrence, Gordon: *Looking at Type and Learning Styles*, Center for Applications of Psychological Type, 1997

- Maddi, Salvatore R.: *Personality Theories: A Comparative Analysis*, Waveland, 2001

- Martin, Charles R.: *Looking at Type: The Fundamentals Using Psychological Type To Understand and Appreciate Ourselves and Others*, Center for Applications of Psychological Type, 2001

- Meier C.A.: Personality: *The Individuation Process in the Light of C. G. Jung's Typology*, Daimon Verlag, 2007

- Pearman, Roger R. & Albritton, Sarah: *I'm Not Crazy, I'm Just Not You: The Real Meaning of the Sixteen Personality Types*, Davies-Black Publishing, 1997
- Segal, Marci: Creativity and Personality Type: *Tools for Understanding and Inspiring the Many Voices of Creativity*, Telos Publications, 2001
- Sharp, Daryl: Personality Type: *Jung's Model of Typology*, Inner City Books, 1987
- Spoto, Angelo: *Jung's Typology in Perspective*, Chiron Publications, 1995
- Tannen, Deborah: *You Just Don't Understand*, William Morrow and Company, 1990
- Thomas, Jay C. & Segal, Daniel L.: *Comprehensive Handbook of Personality and Psychopathology, Personality and Everyday Functioning*, Wiley, 2005
- Thomson, Lenore: *Personality Type: An Owner's Manual*, Shambhala, 1998
- Tieger, Paul D. & Barron-Tieger Barbara: *Just Your Type: Create the Relationship You've Always Wanted Using the Secrets of Personality Type*, Little, Brown and Company, 2000
- Von Franz, Marie-Louise & Hillman, James: *Lectures on Jung's Typology*, Continuum International Publishing Group, 1971

Putting the Reader first.

An Author Campaign Facilitated by ALLi.